What is a habitat? A habitat is a place where things live. A rainforest is one sort of habitat. It is a thick forest where tall trees and lots of different animals live. As you might expect, rainforests get lots of rain!

the tallest trees

canopy

Many of the trees in a rainforest are very tall and grow close together. The tops of the trees make a thick layer called the canopy. Many different types of birds make their homes in this canopy.

rainforest lake

In a rainforest, the air is steamy because it is hot and it rains a lot. On the ground, all that rain forms rivers and lakes.

Rainforests are home to very small birds called hummingbirds. There are many different sorts of hummingbirds. The smallest hummingbird is called a bee hummingbird. It is only 5cm from the tip of its beak to the tip of its tail! The biggest hummingbird is the giant hummingbird, which can be 23cm long.

A hummingbird's wings make a humming sound as they flap.

bee hummingbird

Hummingbirds can hover in one place by beating their wings up to seventy times a second. They flap their wings so quickly that they look like a blur.

Hummingbirds have long bills (beaks) that they use to drink the sweet nectar from deep inside flowers.

a sword-billed hummingbird

One type of hummingbird has a bill that is even longer than its body. The bill is long and thin and looks a little like a sword. This bill gives the bird its name: the sword-billed hummingbird.

Rainbow lorikeets are so called because they have red, yellow, blue and purple feathers. These birds live in tropical rainforests in Australia (/Ostraileeɐ/).

rainbow lorikeet

A rainbow lorikeet is a type of parrot. It is so small that it can fit into an adult's hand.

Rainbow lorikeets fly from flower to flower to eat nectar and pollen. They are also frequently seen on bird feeders in gardens.

young lorikeet

Young lorikeets have black beaks, which turn red as they get older.

Rainbow lorikeets live in pairs. As it gets dark, hundreds of pairs of lorikeets huddle together in tall trees to spend the night.

This bird is a hornbill. Many hornbills nest in holes in trees. They often choose the taller trees that emerge from the top of the rainforest canopy.

female hornbill

The female makes a nest in the hole. She stays in this nest while her mate helps her to close up part of the hole with a mix of mud and poo. They leave a small gap, so the male can give her food. No other animals or predators can get inside the nest.

male hornbill with some food

hornbill nest

gap

The male hornbill brings the female some food to eat. He puts it into the slit in the door.

Inside her nest, the female hornbill lays her eggs. Once the chicks hatch, the male hornbill brings food for the whole family.

As the chicks grow bigger they need more and more food.

The female hornbill pecks down the hard door with her beak. She squeezes out of the hole and then makes a new door from fresh mud and poo. Inside the nest, her chicks will still be safe from predators.

a hornbill getting food

Now the female hornbill also brings food for the chicks. When the young hornbills are ready to get their own food, they peck down the door.

In the Amazon Rainforest, a big bird with pink feathers is looking for food in a lake. The bird is called a spoonbill. It gets its name from its long, flat bill, which looks like a spoon.

spoonbill

bill

pink feathers

The Amazon Rainforest is in South America. It is the biggest rainforest on the planet.

To get food, the bird opens its bill a little. Then it dips its bill into the lake. Next, the spoonbill walks slowly, swinging its head from side to side.

The lake is far too muddy for the bird to see its food, so instead it feels for fish and insects with its bill. When the bird feels a fish, its bill snaps shut to grab the food!

The harpy eagle is a very big hunting bird that lives in the canopy of the Amazon Rainforest.

It flies from tree to tree looking for tree-dwelling animals, like sloths, to eat. When it spots a sloth, the eagle grabs it with its long, sharp claws, called talons. Then it flies up to a tall tree to eat its feast.

The harpy eagle's legs are as thick as a broom handle, and its talons are longer than your fingers.

harpy eagle

A harpy eagle is three feet tall.

The eagle cuts into the sloth's thick fur with its strong, curved beak. Then it tears off chunks of meat.

sloth

curved beak

In the Amazon Rainforest, parrots called macaws live in flocks of up to thirty birds.

The red, yellow, green and blue feathers of macaws might look bright to us, but in fact they help the macaws to hide from the snakes and big hunting birds that want to eat them.

Blue feathers help macaws to hide in the forest's shadows.

Macaws crush hard nut and seed shells with their strong beaks.

Green feathers help macaws to hide in leaves. And red and yellow feathers can look like seeds or flowers.

Macaws feast on seeds and nuts. Sometimes, they eat seeds that contain poison, but the macaws never get sick. Why not?

When macaws eat seeds that have poison in them, they fly to a riverbank or cliff where there is clay in the soil. Then the macaws eat some of the soil. The clay helps the poison to leave the parrot's body. It's like a medicine for parrots!

clay soil